MY
LIFE

The Brandon L. West Story

BRANDON L. WEST

Lightning Fast Book Publishing, LLC
P.O. Box 441328
Fort Washington, MD 20744
www.lfbookpublishing.com

LIGHTNING FAST
BOOK PUBLISHING

Stay Connected with Brandon L. West at www.brandonlwest.com.

The author of this book shares life experiences to aid the reader in overcoming adversity. The information provided is based on the personal philosophy and experience of the author. The intent is to offer general information that, when applied, will aid readers in becoming the best person they can be. In the event that you use any of the information in this book, the author and publisher assume no responsibility for your actions.

The publisher, Lightning Fast Book Publishing, assumes no responsibility for any content presented in this book.

ISBN-10: 0996541101
ISBN-13: 978-0-9965411-0-7

ACKNOWLEDGMENTS

I would like to thank God for giving me the strength to do this book. I thank him for answering my prayers.

I would like to thank my mom, Debra West, for believing in me throughout my life, and believing in this book.

I would like to thank my family for their love and support.

I would to thank Mrs. King, Mr. Horne, and Ms. Graham.

CONTENTS

CHAPTER 1

WE ARE FAMILY

My name is Brandon West and I was born in Hampton, Virginia, at 3:00 pm at Hampton General Hospital on December 15, 1989. I'm the only child born to Debra A. West. I never knew who my father was. The city that I grew up in (Hampton) has a population of 137,000 people. Several events in my life have directed this path depending on the circumstances in which I found myself. Living with my Grandparents Julius West Jr., Julia E. West, my aunt Juliette Williams, my cousins Nicole, Frances, LaRhonda, Natalie, and last but not least my wonderful mom Debra, people still can't believe to this day how all of us lived under the same roof.

My Grandfather was in the Air Force for 28 years, retiring in 1977. He was the father figure I never had. He was a true Man of God who gave me so much advice about life and what to expect. He played a great role at Bayview Chapel and at the Langley Chapel. He was an active singer in the Male Chorus, Mass Choir, and was a Deacon for many years. My Grandfather loved going to the Base Theatre, not only because the food was good, but because it was a lot cheaper than the AMC Theatre and Cinema Café. I remember the time my granddad, Natalie, LaRhonda and I went to go see *Wild Wild West* starring Will Smith and Selma Hayek. We also saw the movie *The Mummy* on the same night starring Brendan Fraser. My grandparents would have date night every Friday or Saturday night. They would have the traditional dinner and a movie kind of date. My granddad was a huge fan of Queen Latifah. Every movie that she was in, we had to see it.

I remember the times my Granddad and I would make those late night Burger King runs. This was back when Whoppers were 99 cents. I miss those days. He used to get the Whooper and fries with his senior citizen drink (orange soda). As for me I would always get the double whooper with cheese, onion rings, and a chocolate milkshake.

My Granddad and I would go to the best barbershop in the city of Hampton, BK's Barbershop. I've been going there since I was 2 years old back in 1991. I'm telling right now to take your sons, grandsons, nephews, and so on to BK's Barbershop. You will not be disappointed. The Barbers' names are Booker, Chris and Charles. I've had people compliment me on my hair for so many years. Ladies, you can get a trim from BK's Barbershop as well – I don't want you to feel left out. Anyway, my Granddad and I would wake up around 7:00 am on Saturday to go to the barbershop, and be the first ones there. The shop opened at 8:00 am. We would always stop at Hardees to get us a sausage and egg biscuit on the way, or sometimes go to IHOP, which was after we got our haircuts. We would sit and wait for Chris to open up. To make a long story short, we looked real good coming out of there. As my grandma would say "you look a thousand times better."

My grandparents were involved in an organization called the Share Program. The Share Program involved going to the food bank and putting together food boxes for families in need. Some we delivered, while other families came to pick them up. I remember when I was little, the first Saturday of every month around 5:00 AM, we would get up and go to the building where they were putting together food boxes. This was my first experience of helping people who were in need. Seeing people happy and content with life as they received these gifts was amazing. The tears of joy I saw on their faces were priceless moments to me. Ever since those days,

I've always given back to people. Whether it was clothes I couldn't wear anymore, shoes I couldn't wear anymore, old watches, etc. I've always told people one thing you need to know about me is not to ever take my kindness for weakness or goodness for granted. If you don't know, now you know. I'm glad they instilled that mindset of blessing somebody else instead of always blessing yourself within me. That was a lesson my grandparents taught me.

People often wonder why God keeps on dropping blessings in my life and in my family's life. The reason is because we bless other people. In the words of my grandmother, "Brandon, this is a give-and-take world. You better be giving to people just as much as you are taking from people." She also said, "Some parents and grandparents teach you how to take, but they don't teach you how to give."

Speaking of my grandmother, she is a great Woman of God, and very blunt at times. If she had something to say to you, she would say it to your face. I remember during my childhood I was always on the receiving end of spankings. I remember touching the hot stove when my grandmother specifically told me not too. My grandma said "Brandon, stay out of this kitchen. I'm cooking right now. I'll call you when everything is ready." So I tested the waters and touched it anyway. I screamed so loud, and my grandmother came in and said, "Didn't I tell you not to touch that stove?" So she got my granddad's belt from one of his church suits and started to whoop me right then and there. I was something else as a child, but I appreciated those spankings because it made me into the great person I am today. There was no such thing as time-out or sit in the corner in the West family household.

My grandmother was the first one to teach me how to cook at the age of 13. It all started with cooking eggs, grits, bacon, pancakes, rice, frying fish, liver and onions, and so on. Also, my grandmother taught me how to wash clothes as well. Every Friday afternoon or early Saturday morning, we would wash clothes together. I remember my grandma telling me "Brandon, whether you get married or not, you need to know how to do for yourself." There were times when my grandmother and I would go shopping early Saturday mornings around 9:00 AM. She would do all her shopping at the Coliseum Mall back in the day. I miss the Coliseum mall. Then we would go have lunch at Piccadilly. That was my Grandparents' favorite place to eat on special occasions such as their wedding anniversary, Father's Day, Mother's Day, Easter, and on birthdays. Piccadilly was the place where my grandmother would take the time to lecture me about life and the future. She would always tell me to keep God first in everything you do. Always be true to yourself, and don't change yourself just because a few people can't handle the beauty they see inside of you.

My grandmother is alive and well at the age of 80. She suffers from dementia, which a lot of elderly people suffer from. I never knew what dementia was until my grandma started to have it. It wasn't very common among black people. She has been through hell and back, as has my grandfather.

Now my mom, Debra West, is my hero. She is the hardest-working woman you will ever meet in your life. She has done a lot for me, and I thank God for her. I appreciate everything she has done for me in my life. My mom and I have laughed together, cried together, had our disagreements, but always still love each other. She works at Langley Air Force Base as the number one Chef on Base. People compliment her all the time about her cooking. My grandparents and I would go to the Officers Club almost every Sunday after church. Even church folks would write me on Facebook asking me, "Brandon, is your mama cooking tonight? If so let me know." My mom has been a chef at Langley Air force Base for 34 years, since 1980.

We have a great bond with each other. My mom is very easy to talk to, and she is very understanding. She keeps it real, just like my grandma does. They love you enough to tell you the truth. I never had a problem communicating with my mom. People would always come up to me saying, "Brandon, I wish I had the same kind of relationship you and your mom have." A lot of young people call her Mama D. She is just that mother figure they never had growing up, or maybe their moms just don't talk to them. She's always giving them advice on relationships, dreams, school, and more. She is a great role model, and I love her very much. There were times when my mom and I would go to the Midnight bowling that they had on base. It was a glow-in-the-dark type of atmosphere. We ate hot wings, fries, and chicken fingers. We always had ourselves a great time. We would also see church folks as well having a great time.

My mom dates a guy named Don. Don is very old-school and country. He got his Bachelor's Degree from Norfolk State University. He is a great guy, and I respect him very much because he has always been there for my mom and I. I remember when Don, my mom, and I went to Danville for the very first time in 2001 to meet his parents, Audrey and Malcolm Coles. I was very nervous because it was my first time going. This was only my mom's second time going. When I got there, they welcomed me with open arms and gave me so much love. I remember Mrs. Coles telling me, "Brandon, help yourself and make yourself at home." Even though she gave me the green light to do whatever I wanted, I still felt like I was walking on eggshells. I didn't want to seem greedy since I was at somebody else's house. I know I'm not the only one who has ever felt this way.

We would visit Danville occasionally. Eventually I felt more comfortable with the family and let my guard down. We would go to Danville the day after Thanksgiving, Memorial Day weekend, Christmas, Independence Day, and Labor Day weekend. Don's younger brother, Victor, was a WWE wrestling fanatic just like me. He would go to Blockbuster and rent *WWE Wrestlemania King of the Ring* shows. We would wrestle downstairs and nobody cared. My mom would say, "Brandon, be careful," and Don would say, "Leave that boy alone."

Victor Coles passed away in 2005 from a heart attack. God bless your soul, Victor, and may you rest in peace. I remember Don's other brother, Reggie, who reminded me of my Uncle Julius, would take his two kids, Jackson and Mckenzie, and I shopping in Greensboro, North Carolina. Greensboro is only an hour away from Danville. He would tell me, "Brandon, whatever you want, I'll pay for it." I went on a crazy shopping spree.

I remember on the days we would leave to go back home to Hampton, Mrs. Coles would always fix fried chicken, eggs, bacon, sausage, grits, and biscuits. The food was delicious. Mr. Coles would always slide five dollars into my hand before I would leave. He would say, "Here you go, you are a great young man." I haven't been to Danville in 8 years. I still keep in touch with them to this very day. I want to go back to Danville in the near future. As you can tell, I've had some great memories with my mom, Don, and his family. They will always have a special place in my heart. I can go on and on about my mom but, I'll stop here for now.

Another great woman in my life is my Aunt Juliette, who is basically my second mom. I love all my aunts so dearly, but she was the closest one to me during my childhood. When my mom wasn't around, I was always hanging out with my aunt. I remember the times she would always stand at the bus stop waiting for me to get off the bus, looking beautiful with her hair and makeup all done up. I remember going to my aunt's church as many times as I went to my own church. The Church was named Christian Soldiers Ministries, which Bishop Billy Williams (who is her husband) and my uncle preached at. I remember mostly Friday and Saturday nights when we would get out of church around 1:00 or 2:00 AM. Those were long nights! Then we would get back up early in the morning for the 11:00 AM service on Sunday. I only went to my aunt's church if my mom was working or if my grandparents were on vacation. It was a great church, so I can't complain.

My aunt is also my hero. She has been through a lot in her life, and is still going strong. My aunt can make a song about anything.

When she is washing clothes she is singing, and when she is cooking she is singing. She has a great sense of humor, but will tell it like it is. My aunt has diabetes, just like my grandfather. It's very common in our family. She has handled it very well, to say the least.

Now for my cousin, Nicole Villifane. She is so hilarious. When I was a baby, she would drive my mom crazy. She always wanted to bathe me and clothe me every chance she got. She is truly the Fashionista of the family. On October 19, 2003, my cousin Nicole took me to Hooters where she used to work to watch *WWE No Mercy PPV*. I remember her husband Rafael came to my house in this nice yellow car. I was very excited to go. He dropped me off at their apartment where I saw Nicole. She told me, "Brandon, you can help yourself. We got leftover Chinese food and pizza in the refrigerator if you want it." I told her, "No thank you." I was too anxious to eat because this was my first WWE PPV. When I got to Hooters everybody was so excited. There were guys chugging down beer, eating hot wings and fries, and the gorgeous women with their nice orange shorts, serving people. I had chicken tenders with fries and a Dr. Pepper. I drenched my chicken tenders and fries with Texas Pete hot sauce. The food was amazing. I remember the show was beginning, and seeing all of my favorite WWE stars wrestle was great. After the show was over, Nicole took me back to my apartment. She and mom talked for a while, and then she went back home.

Nicole and Rafael currently live in Jacksonville, Florida, with their 9-year-old son, Juan Miguel. Juan Miguel is the funniest, most charismatic child you will ever meet in your life. He really does keep you entertained. He has spent the last two summers in Virginia, and I must say we had a great time. Rafael is in the Navy and Nicole is a business woman working with Mary Kay. When it comes to hair and makeup and clothes, ask Nicole. She won't let you down.

Then there was my cousin Frances, who basically is the combination of my aunt, mom, grandma, and granddad all wrapped up into one person. She is the true definition of a virtuous woman. I've had a lot of laughs with her back in the day, and still do. I remember one time when I was very little Frances, LaRhonda, Natalie, and I would go to the Coliseum Mall together. There was this store called Rave back in the day, and that is where my cousins would have a ball shopping. Then we would eat pizza at this place called Sbarro. The pizza was so amazing. My cousin Natalie would always get Chinese food from this place called China Max. Then we would go to the arcade and play Tekken. For those of you who don't know what Tekken is, it's a fighting game with different tournaments.

Every time Frances would come down to visit during the summer, she would invite everybody to Chuck E Cheese, and we would have a ball. Frances is currently living in Italy as a military wife with her Husband, Derek Cobbs, otherwise known as Big D, along with their two sons, DJ and Wesley James. Derek was in the army for 16 years until he retired because of shoulder problems. I remember meeting Derek for the first time back in 2001. He is hilarious. I remember Derek, his son DJ, who is 16 years old now, and I would always go see a Marvel movie every time they came down for the summer. I love them very much. I was honored to be at their small wedding ceremony many years ago.

My cousin LaRhonda is my video game buddy. Both of us have been huge WWE wrestling fans since 1998. I remember when my mom gave me my first game system, the Nintendo 64, on Christmas day in the year 2000. The few games she gave me were *Mario Kart, Super Mario, WWE Wrestlemania 2000, WWE Shut your Mouth, WWE Just Bring It,* and *WWE Here Comes the Pain.* We would play until 1:00 or 2:00 AM in the morning, until my mom came in the room and said, "Go to bed." I was only allowed to play video games on the weekends. Monday through Friday was all about school, except for when the holidays came around.

I remember back in 2006 when LaRhonda and her boyfriend at the time, Michael, took me to see *WWE Smackdown* live at the

Norfolk Scope. I was thinking about bringing an Undertaker sign to the arena, but thought better of it. Michael came to my house and picked me up to go back to their apartment. LaRhonda was inside getting ready and Michael told me, "Go inside and tell your cousin the tickets are in the first drawer." She got the tickets and we hit the road to Norfolk. Traffic was backed up, which we expected, as soon as we got to the Scope. Cops were everywhere telling people to get out of the way. I was so nervous and happy I didn't know what to do. I'm telling you, seeing wrestling live and feeling the energy from the people was amazing. We got back home around 11:00 PM, and I saw myself on TV when they showed the tape on Friday! This was not the only Live Wrestling event LaRhonda and I would go to.

On April 10, 2012, we went to another *Smackdown* show. This time it was at the Hampton Coliseum. I remember leaving Thomas Nelson after taking a test, and rushing to beat the traffic to find a parking space. My seat was in the middle of the Coliseum. I could see everything. While the crew was setting up the ring, my cousin LaRhonda called me saying, "Where are you seated?" I told her, "I'm sitting in the middle, close to the stage." I was looking around the Coliseum, and then I saw her and her friend Keith. They had floor seats to the far left from where I was sitting. I had Popcorn, two hot dogs, and a Sprite. The price of food was high. I could've gone to a 7-eleven and gotten a few snacks for a cheaper price, but I was so hungry that I just didn't care. The show was beginning, and I was hollering at the top of my lungs, just like any other wrestling fanatic. The Big show, Randy Orton, Kane, Daniel Bryan, Roddy piper, Ryback, and more were all there at the Coliseum. I remember after the show was over I had to get my John Cena t-shirts. The line was very long. People were cussing and raising all kinds of hell. I said to myself, "Lord please let me leave this Coliseum safe and sound."

LaRhonda is a great woman and a great person. She is very intelligent. She is in a relationship with a guy named Terrance, and they have a beautiful baby girl named Tiana. She also has four other sons named Jayvon, Jalen, Dajuan, and Deandre. These boys are hilarious. Even though they drive me crazy sometimes, I still love them. They all have their own personalities. Jayvon is the leader who keeps the others in check. Jalen is the comedian, Dajuan is the sensitive one, and Deandre is a laid back kind of kid. He acts like an old man at times. I see them all the time on Sunday for dinner. They always get on my laptop and play these cool math games or play the Wii.

It was my cousin Natalie, who is the baby out of all four of them, who is the one who introduced me to the game called *Tetris*. I love that game so much. I remember when she had her Grey Gameboy back in the day. Before the days of DS or 3DS, Gameboys were very popular. I used to play that Gameboy all the time, until my mom bought me Gameboy Color. It was a smaller version of the original Gameboy. That's when I had the games *Wario Land* and *Tetris*. I also had *Tetris* for my Nintendo 64 as well. Frances, LaRhonda, Natalie, and I would stay up all night trying to unlock codes and pieces to the puzzle. Natalie is a great woman, mother, and wife. She and her husband, Tony, who is another wrestling fan, have three beautiful children named Anajia, Briana, and Demetrius. Anajia is the energetic one, but also fun-loving. Briana is the hilarious one always trying to wrestle you, and Demetrius is the quiet one, but can break out of his shell at any time. Even though I don't see them as much, I still enjoy their presence when they come down to visit.

God blessed me with seven uncles named Julius III, Nathaniel, James, John, Jonathan, Billy, and Julian. They are great men, great fathers, and wonderful husbands. These men have also been my role models just like my granddad was. People would ask me, " How does it feel not knowing your father?" My response to that was, "I never felt sad, but I feel not knowing my father was a blessing because God provided me with great men in my life to fill that role."

Let's start with my Uncle James. This man is so hilarious. He is also my movie/wrestling buddy. He is a single man, has been the Minister of Music at Antioch Baptist Church for 30 plus years, and is still going strong. He plans on moving to Los Angeles in the future. I wish him the best in his future endeavors. I remember back in the 1990s when James took Shannon, Shelbi, and I to Discovery Zone. It's basically like a Chuck E Cheese type of environment. We both are nerds when it comes to Harry Potter movies and Marvel movies. James and I went to go see Harry Potter and the Deathly Hallows Part 2 back in 2011 in 3D. The movie was great, but the 3D was horrible. He talks about it to this very day. We also saw Marvel movies like *The Avengers*, *Captain America*, and so on. Thor and the Hulk are his favorite characters. I remember we saw Thor 2 back in 2013. I must say he really enjoyed it. I truly appreciate my Uncle James. He has done a lot for me over the years. On my 16th birthday back in 2005, he took me to Joe's Crab Shack. We just laughed and crack jokes. He always comes by every Sunday after church for dinner. He's planning on getting a dog in the future.

Then there was my Uncle Julius, who currently lives Charlotte, North Carolina. He's been living there for 13 years and he enjoys it. I remember on July 4, 2002, I made my first trip to Charlotte. I was very excited to be going because it was a getaway from Virginia. I was 12 years old at the time, and my grandmother cooked me some eggs and Grits around 7:00 AM in the morning. Before we left, she prayed for us. It only takes 5 hours to get from Hampton to Charlotte. There wasn't that much traffic on the road, either. At the time, my uncle had this nice burgundy Pontiac Grand Prix car he was sporting. The car had comfortable seats, and we were listening to jazz music on the way.

When I finally got there, I was so happy. I sat on their green sofa and was just observing the place. My cousins Shannon and Shelbi came out of their rooms, and we talked for a little bit while my uncle was bringing in my luggage. Then my cousin Spencer, who was four years old at the time, came out and said "hey" to me. That boy is hilarious and still is to this day. Then my aunt Eleanor came out and hugged me, and we talked for a little while. Later on that night we all went to go see fireworks, and they were beautiful. I remember my Uncle Julius saying to me, "Well Brandon, this is Charlotte." I loved it. The next day we just chilled at the house. Spencer had a basketball hoop in his room. We were just shooting hoops most of the day, and then we played the Xbox in the living room. We played the game *Tekken*, which Spencer is really good at. Aunt Eleanor would cook these delicious nachos for dinner. I can smell those nachos cooking in the kitchen even now. They were so good. The nachos were so hot we had to carry hot pads underneath because the plates were too hot to touch. My aunt had a habit of shopping late at night, so sometimes we would eat dinner around 8:00 or 9:00 PM.

The week after that my cousin Lanya came to the house and took us back to her apartment that she had at the time. We would always play in the pool at her apartment, and had a ball. Her daughter Shania who was two years old at the time, was fun to be around, and still is. Jordyn, who is Lanya's second child, wasn't even thought of yet. A few days later, Uncle Julius took us to Carowinds. It is very similar to Kings Dominion. I wasn't really a roller coaster person at that time. I still had that fear, but not anymore. It was so hot that day. I made sure I carried an extra water bottle. We rode water rides mostly and then the swings. I brought my grandma a light green bear from Carowinds. She was happy when she got it.

The next day my uncle took Spencer and I to get our haircuts. The place was packed. I thought we would never get out of there, but I must say we looked so fresh with our nice haircuts. When we got home, Shannon and Shelbi were playing the Playstation and I decided to join them. They had the very first Playstation. They had games like *VIP*, and *WCW Mayhem*, and *Tekken 2*. After that we would go rollerblading down the neighborhood while rapping to Bow Wow and Romeo songs. I remember I accidently ran into one of the neighbor's mailboxes and broke it in half. Sorry to the person whose mailbox that was!

Sometimes we would go to the park because Uncle Julius at that time was teaching Spencer how to play soccer. I must say he was pretty good. We used to stay up late at night watching animated shows like *Cowboy Bebop*, the *Brak* show, and *Oblongs*, as well as many other shows. Shelbi's favorite show was *COPS*. She would always repeat every word that they would sing in the intro.

One day we got word that my grandmother's father, Arthur Bryant, had passed away at the age of 94. We had to pack and make the 4-hour drive to Savannah, Georgia, for the funeral. We checked into a hotel to get settled and then we went to Aunt Olivia's house to go over the funeral arrangements. My grandparents were staying over at Aunt Olivia's while we were in town for the funeral. Aunt Olivia is my granddad's older sister. She passed away on July 4, 2009. They found her dead inside her house, laying beside her bed. She had been dead for a couple of days, and the side of her face was already decomposed. Before everyone found out she was dead, Uncle Robert, who is my granddad's younger brother, had called the house numerous times before he decided to call the police. After the family went over the arrangements, I went back to the hotel, but this time it was with my mom and Don.

The next day was the funeral, and emotions were running high. We got to the funeral and the place was packed. Great-Granddad had on a nice white suit. He looked very sharp. My Uncle Nat said a few words, and then my Grandmother and her sister Aunt Tiny said a few words. Overall the funeral was beautiful. Great-granddad was buried next to his wife Hilda B. Bryant who passed away in 1994. The next day we went to see Aunt Alice, my grandfather's other sister. She was a nice lady. She lived in a nice apartment but had no AC. Everybody knows that Georgia is blazing hot. The fans that she had were doing next to nothing, and it was miserable. Aunt Alice passed away in the fall of 2009. I was ready to go back to Charlotte. We got back on the road and got home around midnight. I took my shower and went to bed. I really didn't unpack anything because my uncle was planning on taking me back home to Hampton in the next few days. I only stayed in Charlotte for about three weeks. Now I was headed back to Hampton, and this time Spencer went with us. We stopped at McDonalds for dinner. I ordered a Big Mac and fries with a large Coke.

When I got back to Virginia, I was excited to be back home. I told my mom the things that we did, and she was extremely happy. She thanked my uncle for everything. I haven't been to Charlotte in 13 years, but I plan on going back in the near future. I really appreciate my uncle Julius. He has done a lot for me over the years, especially receiving a lot of money from him.

Then you have my Uncle Nat. I have some memories of him as well. Every Thanksgiving, he used to take me to see a movie. One of the movies he took me to go see was *Flubber*, starring the late great Robin Williams in 1997. My uncle was a Minister at Trinity Baptist Church in the past. I remember my grandparents and I would always make the drive to Richmond to hear him preach. We always showed up late because my grandmother would always take forever to get dressed. After the service we always went to a seafood restaurant with my Aunt Lanessa and her family. I can't recall the name of the place, but the food was great. We really enjoyed ourselves. We would do this occasionally.

My cousins Nathan and Nadia are hilarious; great kids with wonderful personalities. I'll never forget when they would come to visit us, we would have our 3DS with us along with Spencer and just play *Mario Kart* all day long, and have ball. I love them all very much, and I wish them the best in their future career paths.

My Aunt Lanessa is a quiet and fun-loving lady. I'm proud to call her my aunt. I had the honor and privilege of being in her wedding back in 1998 as the ring bearer.

My Uncle Jonathan is another great man. He currently lives in Philadelphia. He's been living there for 30 years. In 1997 I had the honor and privilege of being in his wedding. I was the ring bearer. It took place at my Aunt's church, Christian Soldiers Ministries. There is where I met Brittany and Francesca. They were fun to be around, and still are to this day. I recently saw Francesca this past Thanksgiving for the first time in six years. I haven't seen Brittany in ten years, since the family reunion in 2004.

Getting back to my Uncle Jonathan, I never took a trip up there to Philadelphia to visit him so I could try those classic Philly cheese steaks, but I will in the near future. I remember Jonathan would come down for the 4th of July and grill hamburgers and hot dogs for our family cookout. He would always have his traditional white towel on his head when grilling. We would have hamburgers, hot dogs, sweet potato pie, potato salad, macaroni and cheese, BBQ ribs, and more. He has given me great advice over the years. I'm proud to call him my uncle. I met his fiancé, Marcia, on Thanksgiving back in 2013. She is a very nice, very laid back lady. I'm glad he found happiness with her.

My uncle Julian is a hilarious guy. I had the honor of being in his wedding back in 1992. I was the ring bearer once again when he married my adorable Aunt Renetta. They've been together ever since.

My Cousins Jaslin and Brittnie would have their birthday parties either at the house or in another facility. The first one I went to was Jaslin's 16th birthday party that she had at the house. I had a blast. Great food, great fellowship, and great music. My uncle Julian picked me up from the house. He still was still setting up and cooking. I remember he would yell at Jaslin, saying, "Jaslin you need to hurry up and get ready; we got people coming here soon." At the party I met Shekinah, Jonathan, Mrs. Rivers, and I already knew who Breona was. She was in my Spanish 3 class at Kecoughtan High School. We played the egg and spoon race. That was pretty fun. The electric slide is always my favorite dance to do. After the party was over I got a to-go plate, and my Uncle James took me home.

Brittnie had her birthday party, which was put together by Jaslin. Once again the party was so fun. Nobody can put together a party like the West family. This time DJ, James, LaRhonda, her four sons, and I went to the party. The food was good. We had macaroni and cheese, fried chicken, potato salad, deviled eggs, and punch to drink. I love them all with all my heart, and I'm thankful for them.

My Uncle Billy is another man I had the privilege to get to know a little bit more. When I first started Thomas Nelson in the fall of 2008, he was my transportation. He used to own a cab company called Victory Taxi Cab. He would come by the house around 7:30 or 8:00 AM and take my grandfather to dialysis, which was down the street from my school, and eventually dropped me off at school. He was a big help to me when it came to needing a ride. Monday through Thursday were the days I had classes. We would pray inside the cab as we traveled to our destination. We would have laughs, and serious conversations about life, personal issues, school, and everything else. He doesn't have the business anymore due to a lot of restrictions the city has put on cabs. He has Parkinson's Disease. I love him and appreciate him dearly. He and my aunt have been married for 11 years and are still going strong. Then there is my uncle John. I really don't know much about him, but he lives in Williamsburg.

CHAPTER 2

EDUCATION IS THE KEY

In the fall of 1995 my mom enrolled me at Mary S. Peake, which is a school I recommend any parent to enroll their child in. I remember getting on the yellow school bus, and I was very excited about starting school. My bus driver's name was Mr. Smith. I would always sit in the front of the bus to talk to Mr. Smith. He reminded me of Common, the rapper. He was a cool bus driver. I met a kid named Tom on the bus. He was Puerto Rican, and was a pretty cool guy. We would sit by each other on the bus every morning and we would talk about Power Rangers and cartoons and more Power Rangers. This was before the love of wrestling came into my life. Tom was a military kid whose dad was in the Air Force, and they moved overseas. He was the first real friend I ever had.

I remember getting off the bus and going to homeroom. My Teacher's name was Mrs. Arms. She was a nice lady. More and more students were coming into the classroom and were just as scared as I was. Some of them would cry and yell, "Mom, Please don't leave me!"

Mrs. Arms went over the rules of the classroom. She would tell us to stand up and introduce ourselves. I almost peed in my pants. So I got up from my seat and went first just to get it over with. I was sitting on a colorful blue rug and listening to Mrs. Arms read books by Dr. Seuss such as *Green Eggs and Ham*, *The Cat in the Hat*, *One Fish Two Fish Red Fish Blue Fish*, and so on. Dr Seuss was my first memory of learning how to read. Mrs. Arms would read word by word slowly and then would show us what she was reading and showed off the pictures as well.

Halloween 1995 was very exciting to me. Mrs. Arms wanted us to dress up in our favorite animated character. I dressed up as Aladdin. I also brought a toy genie lamp as well. After I left Mary S. Peake, I went to Samuel P. Langley Elementary School (Go Leopards!), the best elementary school in the world. Mrs. Taylor was my first grade teacher. My grandfather took me to orientation before the school year started. He told me, "Brandon, you listen to the teacher. I don't want a bad report." I replied, " I will, Granddad." The first day of school came, and I was just as nervous as I was back at Mary S. Peake. My Bus driver was Mrs. Reid. She would always wear these sporty shades every morning. She was a very nice lady. All my cousins had her as their bus driver in the past. I remember getting off the bus and going to Mrs. Taylor's class.

Mrs. Taylor was in her 60s at that time. I was finding my assigned seat and looking at the alphabet that went across the top of the wall above the chalkboard. It had corresponding objects or animals. It was the most kid-friendly thing in the classroom. We would always watch the *Magic School Bus* before we had recess. I was having a great time with my classmates. We would climb the monkey bars and swing on the swings.

I remember going to the Virginia Living Museum for the very first time in the first grade. I was very excited and my mom went with me on that day. They had beautiful exhibits, great volunteers, and a beautiful outdoor nature walk. I have to say my favorite animals were the foxes, otters, beavers, and birds. We ate lunch outside and my mom packed me a peanut butter and jelly sandwich, Doritos, and a Capri sun. After we ate we got back on the bus and headed back to school. My mom looked at me and said, "Did you have a great time?' I said yes. She said, "Good. I have to go to work now. See you at home." I gave her a hug and kiss and she left.

In the first grade I became citizen of the month for the very first time. Mrs. Haywood who was the principal at the time, would say each name for each grade who made citizen of the month on the announcements. After the announcements, they would tell you to come by the office to receive your certificate and tell you to keep up the great work. One day during recess I was playing on the monkey bars and fell and landed wrong. I fractured my left arm. It was only a hairline fracture and I remember going to the ER and the doctor had to bend my arm back and forth. I was screaming so loud. Then the doctor gave me a beige colored cast, and everyone from school, family, and church signed it. I still have that cast to this very day.

My second grade year at Langley was good. My teacher's name was Mrs. Matthews. She was a very impatient woman with a smart mouth. I must admit she was a great teacher, but her attitude was foul. Mrs. Matthews and my grandmother almost got into it one time. I learned how to write paragraphs and learned how to write in cursive as well. I had difficulty with the cursive writing in the beginning, but eventually I got the hang of it.

I was now entering my third grade year at Langley. In the third grade I made the honor roll for the very first time. My favorite teacher was Mrs. Phillips. She was a 5'2" blond haired freckle faced woman. She was a nice lady and was very soft spoken. Mrs. Phillips had her wedding reception at the Langley Officer's Club many years ago. I must say I was a teacher's pet in her class. I got away with a lot of stuff. Thanks, Mrs. Phillips, for everything!

Entering my fourth grade year in the fall of 1999, my teacher was named Mrs. Covington. I remember little about Mrs. Covington except for the fact that she was a six-foot tall brunette who was a decent teacher. She was also the most lenient teacher I had at Langley Elementary school. She allowed the class to have an abnormal amount of freedom. I remember doing the solar system project. I believe my mom was more excited about it than I was. We had three weeks to do it. My mom and I would go to Paul's

Arts and Crafts to get the foam balls, paint, cover board, and so on. We would stay up until 1:00 or 2:00 AM in the morning doing this project! Mrs. Covington wanted us to present it to the class. Anytime I ever had to present a project, I would be either the second or third person to go up. I just wanted to get it over with. Long story short, I got an A (93%) on the project, which brought my grade up from a C (78%) to B (87%).

My other teacher, Mrs. Chung, who is from Hawaii, was my English teacher. We had to write a letter to her son who was in Kuwait at the time. It was an emotional time for her knowing that her baby was overseas, but he came back home safe and sound. God is good. He made a surprise visit to our class, and he thanked us for the letters that he received from us. Another thing that happened was Music class. For those of you that know me, then you know that I can't sing. I can't carry a tune, but it was a class I had to take. We had Monday night concerts at the beginning of the school year into the Christmas holiday. My aunt Juliette, LaRhonda, Natalie, and Frances would go sometimes. My mom was usually working.

My fifth grade year was very busy. Fifth grade was all about graduation. I was happy that this was my last year at Langley Elementary. I couldn't wait to go to Middle School. Mr. Balod, who was from the Philippines, was my English teacher. His spelling tests were decent. We had about 20 to 25 words to study. Mr. Balod wanted us to do an autobiography about our life. This was our final project grade. We had to present it to the class in alphabetical order. I was the last one to go, and I was going through the anxiety because I wanted to get it over with. He told us we had about five minutes to present, and it seemed like the longest five minutes of my life. Long story short, I got a good grade on it.

Mr. Pipes, who was my science teacher, wore big bifocal glasses. He made science class enjoyable. I remember he took the class to Nauticus, and it was so much fun. I remember we got to touch the horseshoe crabs that they had there. I can't recall my math or history teacher's names, which is sad, but both of those ladies were great teachers. I remember taking the SOL Tests in the fifth grade. These tests were very serious, but it didn't determine whether you were promoted to the next grade or not. That didn't happen until high school. My grandparents were praying for me before the week of SOL testing and during the week of SOL testing. God has never failed me yet. My score in science was 402, English 401, math 402, and history 403. I still made it through.

Mrs. Murray, who was our music teacher, had us go over the songs for graduation. Everyone was already drained from studying and taking the SOL tests, and now you put this on us? The struggle was real y'all. I remember the night before graduation I waited until the last minute to look over these songs. I wasn't really into these songs. All I wanted was my diploma and to move on with life. Graduation day came on June 14, 2001. My grandparents, mom, Frances, and DJ came to the ceremony. Everyone else had to work, but they made up for it by giving me a financial blessing. The auditorium was packed and I can remember Mrs. Murray singing the National Anthem with so much passion. Mrs. Haywood was thanking everyone for coming out and telling us how proud she was of us in making it this far. Then it was time for us to sing. I came to find out we were singing *Tell Them We Are Rising*. It was not one of the four songs she made us stress over to get right and to be prefect on graduation. Mrs. Murray, you were the best music teacher that school ever had. Well that's' the end of my journey from Langley Elementary School.

Now I enter the middle school years. In the fall of 2001 I went to Syms Middle School, and let me tell you it was a whole different atmosphere. I was nervous and happy at the same time. My mom, granddad, and grandma gave me a hug and kiss, telling me, "Brandon, have a great day at school." The bus was packed so I sat all the way in the back, being so quiet. No longer were we riding the yellow school bus, but now we were riding the HRT buses. We arrived at the school and I went to my first block class, which was my history class. My teacher's name was Mrs. Bloom.

She was a short brunette woman with baby blue eyes, and she would tell it like it is.

I'll never forget the day I walked into class and saw Mrs. Bloom crying in her chair. Mrs. Hicks, who was one of the other teachers, came in to comfort her. When all my classmates came in the room after the second bell, Mrs. Bloom and my other teachers came in the classroom and said to us "Guys, we have some bad news. Kenneth Curry passed away over the weekend from an asthma attack." I was so devastated. Kenneth was an easy-going kind of guy. We had many laughs. He sat behind me in class. Kenneth used to tell me, "Brandon, I hate having asthma. I wish it would just go away." Well Kenneth, it's been 13 years since you've been gone. No more pain, hurt, inhaler, and no more struggling you have to go through. Your spirit is free, and may you rest in peace.

Also during my sixth grade year was when the September 11th attacks happened. Once again I was in Mrs. Bloom's class, and she told us the devastating news. It wasn't until I got home that day that I actually saw it on TV. My second class was my English class. My teacher's name was Mrs. Ellis, and she was a fun-loving lady. We would always have Spelling Tests and AR Reading tests in her class, as well as essays to write. Then my third block class was Math with Mr. Riggins. In the beginning, I was getting F's on almost all of his tests. My grandfather would buy me this big Math book from Rite Aid so I could do some practice problems. It was all worth it. I must admit, Math was not my strong subject, but I've gotten better over the years with after-school tutoring and by the Grace of God. Mr. Riggins always made sure you understood the material and was always available to help you when you needed it. I will never forget a teacher like him. I passed his class with a C.

Mrs. Feigh was my Science teacher, and she was a very nice lady. She really had compassion for her students. We would always play Jeopardy when it came to reviewing for a test in the coming weeks. I remember doing a project about Sweet Potato Pie. It was a week before Thanksgiving and she wanted us to pick one of our favorite dishes, and present it to the class. I was very excited about this project. I don't remember the last time I saw Mrs. Feigh, but it's been awhile.

My other class was gym class. My teacher's name was Mrs. Wells. She was a fine looking woman with blonde hair, a nice tan, and a southern accent. I was her favorite and I'm not ashamed to say it. The cool thing about gym class was that I had it during the last period of the day. The guys' locker room was big, but it smelled really bad. I can't stand it when guys don't flush the toilet and don't wash their hands. My locker was number 22, the jacked-up locker. I had gym on Monday, Wednesday, and Friday. I always took my gyms clothes home on Fridays to get them washed and be ready for Monday. Some of the guys I don't believe ever took their clothes home to get washed. Some of them had horrible hygiene and that was *before* gym. In every gym class we would do stretches, push-ups, and jumping jacks. We would have sports day every Friday. Sports day was when you choose any sport you wanted. I would usually pick soccer, tennis, or basketball.

When the gym semester was over, we go right into Health Class with the same teacher, Mrs. Wells, and with the same group of students from my gym class. We talked about serious health issues like cancer, diabetes, strokes, and so on. I remember doing a research paper on diabetes because of my grandfather having it for so many years. I got a 95% A on it. During my 6th grade year, we would have deep discussions about sex. Even though my grandfather had already talked to me about sex, I learned new information. Parents, you must always talk to your kids about sex. Don't try to sugar-coat the truth or rely on the teachers to tell your kids what you should be teaching them at home. I'm glad God gave me people in my life to keep it real with me. A lot of people don't have that. Anyway, we watched videos about sex, and how to protect yourself. They showed us different diseases that you can catch. They brought speakers to come and talk to us about their experiences. I remember one guy who had herpes said he found out he had it when he looked down at his penis while he was in the shower one morning. He told us that many people may have an STD, but the symptoms just haven't shown up yet.

One thing I loved about Middle School were the assemblies, because just getting out of class made my day, and it made the day go by so much quicker. I was now entering my 7th grade year in the fall of 2002. This year was a pretty good year for me. Mr. Jones was my math teacher. He reminded me of my Uncle Nat. He just had a laid back personality, and crack jokes whenever he wanted to. His teaching style was very understanding. He always broke it down for you piece by piece. Mrs. Forbes, who was my History teacher, was a very nice lady. It's funny how teachers would go from teaching class to telling stories about their life that have nothing to do with class. That's Mrs. Forbes for you. I will never forget the time she fell and broke her arm. A classmate named Matt was stretching his legs out and Mrs. Forbes took a few steps back and fell backwards. It was horrible. Tears began to flow and she went to the nurse. We weren't even in class for ten minutes when the incident happened, so everybody was socializing, doing homework, or went to sleep like I did. That's one of the memories I will have of Mrs. Forbes, besides being a wonderful teacher with a great spirit.

My next teacher was Mrs. Dalin. She was my English teacher. She was not a woman to mess with. In the beginning, I didn't like her. I was wondering to myself, "Why is she so freaking mean to everyone?" She would show her nice side once in a while. I remember doing AR reading again just like I did in the 6th grade. It was fun, but very challenging at this point. The books were harder than before. So basically we would have these little cars posted on the wall outside of her classroom to keep up with the score that we had. The papers that we wrote were not as bad as I expected them to be. As for me, I always waited until the last minute to do the papers, but managed to get good grades on them.

Last but not least was my Science teacher, Mrs. Fiest. She was a pretty blonde woman with a decent personality. Every class period we would start with warm-up exercises. They were basically mini lab reports. They were okay, if you ask me. One time a student rubbed Mrs. Fiest the wrong way. He called her a bitch because she told him he couldn't turn in one of the homework assignments that he had at least two weeks to do. She said to him, "There is no excuse for you not to have done this assignment, and it's not fair to all the other students who turned theirs in on time." The student walked out of class and never came back. I remember my first Report Card I had in the 7th grade. I had three Cs, a D and two Bs. I got a D in Math, so once again I went to tutoring after school with a lady named Mrs. Cave. Mrs. Cave reminded me of Mrs. Matthews from my church. Mrs. Cave tutored me and 5 other students every Tuesday at 3:30. Long Story short, I managed to pull my D up to a B. The group math project that we did in class made it go up. My elective classes remained as Bs and my other classes remained as Cs.

I remember these two guys got into a fight in the hallway over some chick that could care less about either of them. All she cared about was that these two guys were fighting over *her*, and now she felt like she was worth something. To all the ladies out there, love yourself and know your worth as a woman.

As I entered my last year at Syms Middle School in the fall of 2003, I must say that this was a great year for me. Even though a few incidents happened, it was still a great year overall. My Math teacher was Mr. Hinds. He was the best math teacher I ever had. All the female students loved him because he looked liked Morris Chestnut, but was even huskier-looking. His classroom was outside in the trailer. There is where I met my buddies Orlando and Ervin. These two guys were hilarious. The three of us were Mr. Hinds' favorite students. Even though he never said it, he showed it. I will never forget one time in class Ervin got into a fight with another classmate. I can't recall what the student's name was, but the fight came out of nowhere. I was sitting two seats behind them when it happened. That was too close for comfort. It happened so fast. All

I heard was an exchange of words and then the fists started flying. I got out of my seat and ran so fast to Mr. Hinds' desk. I can hear Ervin screaming saying, "Get off me man." I saw Mr. Hinds get up from his chair trying to stop the fight. He was yelling, "Break it up guys right now. I said break it up!" Ervin was so mad that he took his shirt off. Mr. Hinds was so disappointed in Ervin because Ervin was one of his favorites. Mr. Hinds sat Ervin down and was talking to Ervin for a few minutes. He was like a father figure to him. Ervin always let people push his buttons. That's why it was so easy to get to him. I used to tell Ervin to control his emotions and just walk away. It's not worth getting suspended for 10 days. He'd been on the Honor roll all year long, so why mess that up? Ervin is doing great now. He has a couple of kids and is doing quite well for himself.

Anyway, back to Mr. Hinds. His teaching skills were great. I managed to get an A in his class by the grace of God. Sometimes Mr. Hinds would tell us stories about his family. His mom is from Jamaica. He showed us a picture of his mom and his fiancé at the time. He told us a story of how he mixed laxatives with brownies and served it to his family!

Mr. Alexander, who was my science teacher, was another funny guy. He was a nice man with a big belly. I used to love watching *Bill Nye the Science Guy* in his class. He made science so much fun. One of the memories I have of his class was when a guy by the name of Nathan brought a toy gun to school. It was a camouflage toy gun, and it fell out of his pocket. Mr. Alexander walked up to us and said, "Whose is it?" I told him it wasn't mine, and obviously Nathan was going to deny it. Mr. Alexander said, "You guys have put me in a bad position because I like the both of you." So he had no choice but to send us to the Assistant Principal's office. So the Assistant Principal sat us down and said, "Ok, I'm going to make this nice and easy, fellas. Whose toy gun is it?" I said, "Sir, it wasn't mine." Once again Nathan denied it. Then the principal looked at Nathan and said, "Why are you crying?" Nathan finally broke, and said, "Ok, ok it was mine. I'm sorry for lying." He also apologized to me for putting me in that position and causing danger towards me and our other classmates. Then the principal said to Nathan, "What in the world were you thinking bringing something like this to school? What if it was real?" The Assistant Principal looked at me and said, "Mr. West, you can go back to class, and Nathan you come with me. We are going to make a phone call." So I rushed to my third block class with Mr. Hinds. He looked at me and said "Brandon, I knew it wasn't you and I'm glad everything worked out alright." So Mr. Alexander came to me the next day and said, "I'm sorry for accusing you." I said, "It's ok."

Now to my Civics teacher, Mrs. Pence. She was hilarious to me. She was a great role model to all of us. She was super cool, and if you were having a bad day, she knew a way to make you happy again. I always looked forward to coming to her class. Mrs. Pence made Civics class so much fun. I remember we turned the entire classroom into a courtroom environment. It was a case about smuggling drugs or something. I was one of the members of the jury, which was an easy grade. I remember a guy by the name of David was the Bailiff and a girl by the name of Mercedes was one of the Lawyers. It was a great experience. We ate a lot in that class. I remember her giving us ice cream and popcorn while we were watching movies. Whether it was related to history or not, she didn't care. There was another Brandon in my class as well. He was a tall kind of guy. He was pretty cool to be around. He and this guy Darius were best friends.

Tragedy struck during my 8th grade year. I remember a guy by the name of Joshua Sechrist. He was a wonderful guy with a great heart. He passed away on January 9, 2004. He loved hockey and hockey was his passion. I wasn't around him much, but when I was, he was always nice to me when we saw each other. His hockey jersey is at the Plaza Roller Rink as a tribute to him. God bless your soul Joshua, and may you rest in peace.

Then there was my English teacher, Mr. Duncan. He was a quiet man. He had a lot of patience with us, and I thought he was a great teacher. Mr. Duncan would always play Tupac on the radio while we would do homework assignments in class. One time he was rapping to Eminem's classic song *The Real Slim Shady*. Everyone was saying, "GO DUNCAN, GO DUNCAN." I remember watching a movie call *House of Dies Drear*. It was a very interesting movie with a supernatural element to it. I did not know that Tichina Arnold from *The Martin Show* and *Everybody Hates Chris* was in it, and as well as Kadeem Hardison from a *Different World*. You learn something new every day. When Mr. Duncan wasn't in class, there was a lady by the name of Mrs. Shoemak. She was a 5'2" feisty Latino woman, but had nice qualities as well. She would always snore in class while we were taking a test. Me and the other students would just laugh at her. She would wake herself up and say, "What the hell is so funny?"

Well, middle school was a great experience for me. I learned not to waste your time trying to impress others. Also don't be afraid of looking weird, and I know it's a cliché, but be yourself, and love yourself. Don't label people. If you do, you could miss out on some amazing friends. Life is painful, and all you can do is learn from it.

In the fall of 2004 I started my first year of high school at Kecoughtan High School. Most of my family went to that school. My Aunt Juliette was the only one who didn't go. She went to Pembroke High School. Freshman year was the beginning of it all. It was a lot different than anything I'd ever been through. I remember waking at 6:00 AM. I took a shower, ate breakfast, and put on my new clothes as I got ready for my first day of high school. I had on my Timberland shirt, blue jeans, and my Timberland boots. I was looking good. At the tender age of fourteen, everyone enters a new chapter in their life. Scared and nervous, you go to high school not knowing what to expect. Everyone is so different. The school was so much bigger than middle school. You may consider yourself a worthless freshman to all the upperclassmen. My mom took me to school and as I got out of the car and went to the main entrance of the school, I paused and took a deep breath. I saw the seniors overpowering the rest of the students in the hallway. Everyone knew I was a freshman, and it made it seem like I was trying too hard. I noticed there were a lot of people bigger than me, and it was kind of scary at first. I saw a few familiar faces from middle school and began to socialize with them for a little bit. I went to Homeroom where my Math teacher Mrs. Furches, who was from Russia, explaining the Syllabus to us. Everyone knows on the first day of school that teachers talk about what we're going to do and blah, blah, blah. I sat in front of this guy named Noah and he was hilarious. Mrs. Furches told us to have our parents sign the syllabus for our first grade.

I'll never forget one time when Mrs. Furches accused me of skipping class for a week. So I had to go the Dean of Boys and get things straightened out. I almost got into an argument with the guy because I knew that I didn't skip class at all. A few days later, I walked into class, and Mrs. Furches came up to me and said, "Brandon, your name is cleared. I went to the Dean of Boys and told him that it wasn't you who was skipping class. You can relax now and tell your mom that everything is straight."

My second block class was with Mrs. Elder, my Honors English teacher. Mrs. Elder was an easy-going lady, but if you crossed her it was over. I remember reading the book *Animal Farm*. The book was great, but the movie wasn't all that good in my opinion. Mrs. Elder is now teaching in Newport News. Then it was lunchtime. I walked fast to the cafeteria to make sure I was first in line. I had pizza and fries for lunch. I sat with Orlando during lunch and we just talked about how our first day was going. Ervin went to Phoebus High School. Anyway, a fight breaks out between two girls. Who gets into a fight on the first day of school? I will never understand it. Here comes Mr. Baker, our Principal, and a few other teachers to break up the fight. The girl couldn't relinquish her grip that she had on the other girl's hair. She pulled some weave out of her hair, and a little bit of her real hair as well. All I could see was a bald spot on her head when they were being escorted from the cafeteria. I remember one of the teachers yelled, "Everybody sit down, now!" By that time lunch was over already. That day I realized what to expect for the next four years.

My next class was Geography with Mr. Botwinick. He was cool and very laid back. He went over the syllabus on what we had to do and then he put in a movie called *Dr. Strangelove or How I Learned to Stop Worrying and Love the Bomb*. In reality, nobody really cared about the movie. I didn't know that James Earl Jones was in it, and that it was his first movie back in 1964.

My Earth Science teacher was Ms. Fuhs. She made everything in class fun and easy to understand. She made everybody feel comfortable. Ms Fuhs would allow you to redo a test if you wanted to. She was just an awesome Science teacher. My next class was Gym with Ms. Rosado. She was a beautiful Puerto Rican woman. In the beginning of class we did warm-up exercises, and then went outside to run laps. I must admit I did have a little crush on her, but who in gym class didn't? After gym class was over, I caught the bus home and told my grandparents who were watching *Maury* about my day. My mother was at work so I sent a text to her about it.

Entering my sophomore year in 2005, I knew how things worked around Kecoughtan. When I walked through the main entrance this time, I had a little bit more confidence. My Biology teacher, Coach Sapp, was an amazing guy and the best science teacher in the world. There was never a dull moment in his class. I remember dissecting a frog for the very first time. It was pretty cool, to say the least. As I was cutting the frog's stomach, I noticed there were still eggs inside her. My partner, Danny, was grossed out about the entire experience. I remember watching *Lorenzo's Oil* in his class. That was a great movie. His tests and quizzes were super easy. Coach Sapp retired in 2008, the same year I graduated.

My Geometry teacher was Mrs. Simpson. Geometry was okay. It had its easy parts, and hard parts as well. Mrs. Simpson always reminded me of Linda Hunt who played Hetty in *NCIS Los Angeles*. Mrs. Simpson was hard of hearing in her old age. Bless her heart. There wasn't a class period where we didn't eat popcorn. I've never met anyone who loved popcorn so much as Mrs. Simpson did. I must admit she would always go the extra mile for you. She said to us, "I will treat you just like I treat my grandkids."

Coach Green was my Gym teacher for the first semester. He was a short guy with big bifocal glasses, and had a deep voice. He was a very simple man. I remember us playing volleyball, baseball, basketball, soccer, and so on. I don't see how people can fail Gym. Just participate and dress the part. Whether you are good at the sport or not, you can at least try.

I took Drivers Ed class with Coach Hebert during my second semester. It was a great experience. We talked about drinking and driving, and texting while driving. We also discussed other serious consequences that could happen if we were careless on the road. We would do a lot of worksheets in his class. He showed us these videos of two teenage boys who lost control of their vehicle, and hit a pole because of drinking and driving. My granddad would always tell me, "Brandon you have to drive for yourself *and* everyone else." I eventually got my license in the fall of 2009 at the age of 20 years old. Anyway, back to Coach Herbert. He was a great teacher and I thank him for everything.

My World History Teacher was Mr. Willoughby. He reminded me of the comedian George Burns. He was an elderly gentleman and talked about his experiences of being in the war. He had a great sense of humor. His classroom was outside in a trailer. Mr. Willoughby only taught for about 45 minutes. He would always say, "Give me your time and attention and the remainder of class is all yours." He taught his class like a college professor. He always challenged us to be better, and he never assigned pointless busy work to us. If you were one of his favorite students, he would always pick on you in class as well.

In the fall of 2006, my Junior year had arrived. I finally made it to be an upperclassman! I believe by far this was the best year for me. Life was amazing for me, and everything was going well. Even though I had some tough classes, I got through it with excellent grades. I had Mr. Crawford for my Art class. He was a wonderful and brilliant art teacher. He always put forth creative projects, and he would inspire you to have new ways of thinking. He was very easy-going and fun to interact with.

I took Spanish 2 class with Mrs. Lopez. She was the most lenient Spanish teacher there was at Kecoughtan. We would play Spanish Jeopardy in her class before every test we were going take in the coming weeks. She made Spanish class fun. I remember learning the differences between such Spanish verbs as estar and ser, tener and venir, and so on.

Having Study Hall was a blessing to me – a great time for me to finish some of my homework, do work that I missed when I was absent, talk to my teachers about my grades, and so forth. There were times when I would just sleep in Study Hall, especially on Mondays. I forget the guy's name who was monitoring Study Hall. He was a big guy, though, with a big belly. He was cool and laid back.

I have to say that one of my favorite teachers during my Junior year was Mrs. Lassiter. Mrs. Lassiter was my Virginia and US History teacher. She made history interesting, and often unpredictable. She was the first teacher to spark my interest in history. I remember watching the movie *Glory* starring Denzel Washington, Morgan Freeman, and Matthew Broderick. It was an amazing movie. It showed the history of African American men fighting the war, and it also showed me how far black people have come as a race.

My other favorite was Mrs. Lay. Mrs. Lay had a big personality, and made English class very fun. It was also the turning point of writing for me. I wrote a lengthy research paper on *MacBeth* by William Shakespeare. I had trouble staying focused on my thesis at times, but thank God a bit of drafting was involved and my final paper was a success. I remember reading the book *To Kill a Mockingbird*. The characters were interesting, and the plot flowed very well. We watched the film adaptation of *To Kill a Mockingbird* starring Gregory Peck and Robert Duvall. It was a pretty good movie.

My Ecology teacher was Mrs. Raman. She is from India. Mrs. Raman made Ecology fun and interesting, studying how animals interact with their environment and with each other. It's very cool studying about wildlife, and it's also very difficult to do. You barely even talk about Biology and Physiology except for when it relates to the predator and its prey. I still see Mrs. Raman to this very day at Planet Fitness. As my Junior year came to an end, I finally realized that I had one year left, and I wanted to make the best of it.

In the fall of 2007, my last and final year at Kecoughtan High School, I had a breath of fresh air that year. I remember my grandfather was getting ready for dialysis, and he looked at me and said, "Congrats, Brandon, on making it this far. We are proud of you." My mom had already left for the dining hall around 5:00 AM, but she texted me later on to give me some words of encouragement. As I walked through the main entrance of Kecoughtan, I remember saying to myself, "One last round." Seeing all the new freshmen coming in looking scared and nervous just like I was three years before. I remember helping this guy find his class, and told him a little bit about the school. I told him that these four years would go by quick for him, and good luck in his studies.

My first class was Math with Mr. Lang. He was a great guy and a great teacher. He gave homework almost every night. If you needed the extra help, he would give it to you. I took a lot of notes in his class, and we were allowed to do homework after he finished teaching.

I took a Co-op class, and my teacher's name was Mr. Hall. Mr. Hall was a hilarious guy, and a guy that will actually teach you something about life. He was one of my favorite teachers at Kecoughtan. I remember we used to listen to the Temptations, James Brown, and the Four Tops while we did our work in class. He would tell stories about his childhood, and how he got into a lot of fights back in the day. I remember one story that he told us was about a guy chasing him down the neighborhood. Mr. Hall said he picked up a brick, and was hiding beside his house. As soon as the guy was coming around the corner running full speed, he hit him in the face with the brick. He was a great mentor and a father figure to a lot of people.

My Government teacher was Mr. Mingee. He had a nice personality. As long as you gave him the right amount of respect as he has given you, everything was good. I really recommend anybody who will be a raising senior to take his class. He's an awesome Government teacher. Moving on to my English teacher, Mrs. Crosby, she was a very spiritual woman. Mrs. Crosby always had a Slurpee in class. She always told us she doesn't drink wine anymore to calm her nerves, so she now drinks Slurpees as a replacement. I remember reading about Beowulf. It was very interesting, to say the least. We watched the movie in class, but the movie wasn't all that great in my opinion.

Mrs. Ray was my Spanish 3 teacher. She was tough as nails, but had a gentle side to her as well. She was in the Army before she started teaching. Mrs. Ray and I joked a lot in class. Senior year went by so fast. Homecoming rallies, coronation, juniors vs. seniors war, and prom had come and gone in the blink of an eye. When I look back at my senior year, I have no regrets. I remember when graduation was approaching, I went to pick up my cap and gown and felt a sense of accomplishment. As I was walking down the hallway with my cap and gown in hand, one of the janitors looked at me and said, "Young man, you deserve it." I said, "Thank you, sir." I took senior pictures during the summer of 2007. When I told my family I was graduating with Honors, they were very excited. I had to go to Mrs. Lay, who was the head of the Senior Committee, and ask her for extra tickets for my graduation. A lot of my family members were coming to my graduation, except for Uncle Julian, who had to work, and Uncle Julius because my cousin Shelbi was graduating on the same day as me! She was graduating in the morning, and I was graduating at night. She lived in Charlotte, North Carolina at the time.

Graduation Day came and I was excited. Emotions were running high and seeing my family there was priceless. When they called my name, I said to myself, "Yep, this is it." I could hear my family cheering me on. Mr. Baker got up and told us how proud he was of us. He wished us luck in our future endeavors. He finished his speech with his favorite line that he always used after announcements. It was, "Make it a great day or not; the choice is yours." After graduation was over, my family and I were taking pictures. The next day was my graduation party. It was a beautiful day outside and I still couldn't believe I was a high school graduate. We had potato salad, macaroni and cheese, BBQ ribs, corn on the cob, hamburgers, hot dogs, and also my graduation cake. A lot of people passed out cards, money, and gave some words of encouragement. My cousin Derek took my granddad and I home after the party was over.

High school had been the greatest four years of my life. Every experience that I had gone through during my time at Kecoughtan was great. From the very first day of high school, being nervous and somewhat scared of what to expect, down to the last. High school will and can be the greatest experience of your life. Make yourself the best person you can be. Have your own identity, affirm yourself, and most of all love yourself.

In the fall of 2008 I started my first year at Thomas Nelson Community College. Just like I felt when I started high school, I got the same feeling when I was a freshman in college. One thing about college is that the teachers could care less if you showed up to class or not. After all, the money's coming out of *your* pocket, not theirs. The teachers get paid regardless.

Starting college affected many of my habits, particularly my study habits. The first couple of months of classes went by smoothly and I actually felt like I was adjusting to everything just fine. I attended class regularly, and took a lot of good notes from the lectures. I already knew that college was a lot different from High school, but continued doing what I was used to doing. My first semester grades came in and I got two Bs and two Cs. I realized on that day that college requires more time management with my study habits – a valuable lesson I would take in for my future semesters. My major is Information Technology. My mom also went back to school to finish her Bachelor's degree and maybe she will continue on for her Master's, which is another blessing. I wish her the best. Love you, mom!

CHAPTER 3

LET THE CHURCH SAY AMEN

I grew up in a small church called Bayview Chapel in the 1990s. It was a nice-looking church with a nice red carpet, red seat cushions, and red curtains. We all know the crazy stories about being forced by our parents and grandparents to go to church every Sunday. There are many young people who believe that going to church is a waste of time. Why would they look at Church like that? Could it be that they don't understand the meaning? Or maybe they think Sunday is our rest day. There are a lot of people that enjoy going to church on Sunday because they understand the concept behind it, and feel as if it's a way to express themselves. I can truly say that I've been on both sides of the situation. I was one of those people that thought Sunday was a day to sleep instead of going to church.

Now, Sunday is the day I get up out of my bed at 7:30 AM and go to Bethel Church. You are probably thinking to yourself, "Why in the world would he get out of bed so early to go to church every Sunday and listen to a pastor preach a long, boring sermon?" To answer your question, church is therapy for me and for my life. I truly believe that we should bring back the teaching of religion in schools so that the young people can see that there are better things to do in life than violence and being behind bars. You don't need drugs and other stuff to make you feel better or cool. The laws want to take prayer out of the schools, but can't figure out why there is so much hell going on in the school systems. I think there is a great chance that if we brought back God in our schools, then that would make the schools a better place to learn, and not have so many problems.

Now back to Bayview Chapel. My Grandparents took me to church six weeks after I was born. Everybody was in amazement about the first grandson in the West Family. My grandmother once told me that everyone wanted to hold me because I was so precious. Two weeks later, I was christened at Bayview. My Godparents are Mr. and Mrs. Simmons, and Mr. and Mrs. Barber. Mr. Barber couldn't make it to the christening because he had to work. As I got a little older, I finally realized how things worked around the church. Mr. and Mrs. Cobwell, and Mrs. Franklin, would always do the Praise and Worship every Sunday. Guys, let me tell you something, they can sing, and I mean sing. I always said that Mr. Cobwell sounds like Luther Vandross when he sings. Mrs. Barbara Rivers would always do the announcements every Sunday, and she stills does it to this very day. The Acolytes were amazing. I remember them wearing these white robes, walking down the aisle and lighting the candles. Whenever my Grandparents would sing in the choir, I would always sit by a woman by the name of Mrs. Helena Meekins. Mrs. Meekins was the preacher's wife. Her Husband was Chaplain Lorenza R. Meekins. He was a short, bald-headed, light-skinned man from Richmond. He was a really nice man, but I must say his sermons were very long! I don't know how many times I fell asleep in church when he would preach. He was an awesome Chaplain, though. Mrs. Meekins would always call me her baby. I was one of her favorites. Mrs. Meekins passed away January 1, 2014, on New Year's Day. God rest your soul, Mrs. Meekins, and may you rest in peace. Two other ladies I use to sit by were Shandette and Ann Harper. They knew my mom from the days of going to the Officers Club on base to eat. They were very sweet, and still are to this very day. I really appreciate the both of them.

It seems I was always on the receiving end of a butt-whooping in church. Grandma would take me outside and she would get the belt and whoop me right in front of the church. Like I said before, I'm glad I received those whoopings because if I didn't, I honestly think I'd be on the wrong side of the law today. I truly believe we need some of that old-school discipline in this generation. Since when is whooping your child with the belt considered abuse? If that's the case, then every mama, grandma, and aunt out there would be locked up.

There were times when my Grandparents would sing at the base theater. It was some sort of Gospel Explosion where different choirs would come out and sing. They would always have food right across the street at the Community Center. They served green beans, fried chicken, potato salad, macaroni and cheese, rolls, and soda or punch to drink. Once a month, Mrs. Rivers would say in church, "If anyone has a birthday, could you please stand up?" I was so shy back then, and didn't have the confidence to speak in front of a group of people yet, so my granddad would always speak for me. Bayview Chapel was a great church.

Word got around that we had to leave the church because there were people planning on making the church into a storage room. A lot of people were upset about it, including my grandparents, but they finally came to accept the reality of it. We eventually moved to the Langley Chapel in the new Millennium. The church was a lot bigger and it had more seats. My cousin DJ was with us during our first service at Langley Chapel. Change is always good. Sometimes you need to get out of your comfort zone to grow. My grandfather told me, "Brandon, it's time for you to start doing some activities in the church." I already knew I couldn't sing, so the choir was off my list. I decided to join the Usher Board. Ushers play a big role at church. It's not all about helping people find their seat, but also helping them have the right frame of mind. Mrs. Cherry ran the Usher Board. She was the President of the Usher Board but has since retired from what I understand.

I would usher every second Sunday of each month. We wore black and white. The people that I worked with on second Sundays were Mrs. Revells, Mr. Tibbs, Jordan Crawford, Brandon White, Mrs. Dawn Locke, Mrs. Griffin, Mrs. Dowling, Mrs. Issac, and the late great Mrs. Betty Ball. I Loved being an usher, and I am happy that Mrs. Cherry gave me the opportunity to be one, as well as God.

We would always have our Ushers' Breakfast at Golden Corral. My grandmother and I would always go to this event. You can never turn down a free meal that the church has already paid for! A guest speaker would come and give the word. After everything was over, some people left or others just continued to eat more and talk.

Dawn Locke passed out one time in church. It was a very hot day and we passed out so many fans that we almost ran out. Some folks were fanning themselves with the bulletin or brought a mini fan with them to church. Ms. Dawn was laying on one of the pews in the back, and people were fanning her waiting for the ambulance to come. I could hear Chaplain Burrell saying, "Everyone, start praying!" Ms. Dawn came back to church the following Sunday.

The Usher board always treated us young people really well. I remember we went to the Plaza Roller Rink. They were showing us appreciation for our services as ushers. I will never forget the unforgettable moment when Allison took a huge fall at the skating rink. It was hilarious. I was an Usher from 2000-2010. It was a great experience. In 2004 I joined the Drama Guild. Mr. Plummer and the late great Mr. Ross were heads of Drama Guild. Mr. Plummer begged and pleaded so many times for me to join the Drama Guild, and I always said no. He finally convinced me to do this play called *Never Bargain with the Devil* in February 2005. My character was called Love 1. I was so nervous about doing this play. We had the play at the Community Center and the place was packed. My mom, grandparents, and my aunt Juliette and uncle Billy came to support me in this big event. The play went well and everyone gave us a standing ovation. I must say that the youth plays we did were so much better than the adult plays! After my first play went well I did fourteen more plays until my last one in July 2008. We would always do plays in February, July, and November. Even though this was my first time in the acting field, I must say I was an okay actor. My acting was decent enough to get by. Being in the Drama Guild taught me to be more confident, and it helped me in speaking in front of large crowds. I do not have a problem with speaking in front of people now thanks to the Drama Guild. The other thing I've learned is that it's not easy to be on stage acting in front of people, and it's tiring. I really have a deep respect for stage actors and performers now because of their passion for the arts and their commitment to what they do. I would like to thank both Mr. Plummer and Mr. Ross for letting me be in the Drama Guild. I really miss Mr. Ross and his funny sense of humor. It's been two years since he's been gone. God rest your soul, Mr. Ross, and may you rest in peace.

Another great man of god who is no longer with us is Clarence "Mr. Flip" Wilcox. He was under the PYOC, which stands for Protestant Youth of the Chapel. He was great man. I remember him being responsible for the Kings Dominion trips that we would have every summer in the month of July. He was also a great Bible Study teacher as well. God bless your soul, Mr. Wilcox. Rest in peace.

I haven't been to Langley Chapel since 2011. I've been going to a church called Bethel Church. I wanted to experience something different. I grew up in the black church, but I'd never been to a multicultural church before. Meeting new people from different races, backgrounds, and so on was incredible. I love seeing other people praising God differently from what I am accustomed to. I've been going there for 9 months now. I love going to their early service. We are only in church for an hour.

One thing that I have learned about the church is that there are some great Christian people, and then you have those who show nothing but disrespect inside the church. I've witnessed some people in the church hating on one another, rolling their eyes at other people's accomplishments, backstabbing others, bullying others, lying to others, trying to demoralize others. Sometimes the church has more drama than the *Atlanta Housewives*! Now you may be asking yourself, "Does this kind of behavior really happen in the church?" Of course it does! This is the reason why people speak negatively about the church. It's very difficult to bring people to church for the first time, or bring people back to church, and for people to actually take church seriously when negative behavior like this happens. It's very hurtful for people when others in the church are setting examples in such a nasty and disrespectful manner. That can create some bitterness for some people. We need to bring the love and compassion back into the church again. When people come to visit your church, they are not only looking for a church home. Most of them are also just observing how church folks really act. You have people who are trying to get closer to God, and have a relationship with God, but the problem is they keep on running into people who are full of you-know-what. The old folks used to say that the church was like a hospital. Well, we need to help the people who are wounded instead of adding more wounds to them. Let's make them feel comfortable, happy, joyful, and make them look forward to coming to church on Sunday. Don't get me wrong. I'm not saying every church is perfect. Every church has its issues, but we got to do better. I'm not telling you to stop going to church. But when you go, decide to block out all the negativity that people want to bring and focus on God. God wants the church to be a place of love and encouragement. It's supposed to be a place where we build each other up, where we inspire one another to do better in their lives, and to love more deeply. Don't worry about all the negative gossip they say about you in the church. God will deal with them later on his terms. Yes, church may be a place where you've been hurt, but it can also be a place where you can heal from the past. It can be medicine for your deep wounds. If you are one of those individuals who has been hurt in the church, I would like to say I'm sorry that you had to go through that. I would like for you to find a great congregation that can provide you with the support and healing that you've been unable to find all these years. It's bad enough that people get treated like crap by the world. They don't need to come to church and be treated the exact same way.

CHAPTER 4

WHEN HELL KNOCKED ON MY DOOR

In order to understand life we must first go through some sadness and pain that scars our hearts. To me, everyone comes out wiser, but just don't show it. In the words of Dolly Parton, "If you want the rainbow you got to put up with the rain." One incident that occurred was on Halloween, October 31, 2003. It was a Friday, and I was getting ready for school. I was in the eighth grade at the time, and I remember my grandma and I had plans to go to the Halloween Extravaganza at Bethel Manor Church. I was very excited and couldn't wait to go. When I got home from school, my mom was in the kitchen doing dishes, and my grandmother was nowhere in sight. I asked my mom, "Where is grandma at?" She looked at me and said, "Brandon, your grandmother fell and broke her hip in the parking lot at Food Lion. We won't be going tonight." I was devastated and paralyzed with shock. My granddad was at dialysis at the time and he was in tears. Every single day I would go to Sentara Hospital after school to visit my grandma. I would sit in my Grandmother's room doing homework while watching the nurses come in and out of the room to check her vital signs. I got so sick and tired of eating hospital food almost every day! Don't get me wrong; the food was good but I was done with it. Seeing my grandmother in pain was not a pretty sight. Any time the doctor would touch her leg or tell her to move it herself, the screaming and shouting would happen. The family would come over after church or before they went to work to see how she was doing. I remember Chaplain Dicks, who was the chaplain at the time, came to see her as well as some members from the Langley Chapel. At the time we didn't ask for many visitors until we were good and ready. My grandmother had different times of the day where she would do leg exercises as well as walking up and down the hallway. I was so happy when she home. She came back to church that Sunday and everyone was happy to see her. Mrs. Penny gave my grandma the microphone, and she began to testify about her journey through rehab and how far God had brought her.

Another Incident that occurred was when my grandfather almost bled to death. It was in October 2005, around 12:00 AM at night. I was upstairs sleeping and my grandmother was upstairs watching TV in her room. I heard a loud scream from my granddad screaming, " Julia, Julia, Julia!" which woke me up. I jumped out of bed, and both my grandma and I rushed downstairs to see what was happening. What we saw was very graphic. There I saw my grandfather standing in front of the mirror in the bathroom while blood was shooting from his arm. It was the arm that they did Dialysis on, and he had ripped the bandage off too hard. Blood was all over the sink, mirror, floor, and walls. It was very disturbing, and it looked like a crime scene from *CSI*. My grandma called my mom and aunt shouting on the phone saying, "Hurry up and get here quick, your father is dying!" I called 911 and the ambulance came in 5 minutes. Thank god the ambulance was right down the street from my house. When the ambulance came, I had already laid my grandfather on the floor because he was already weak from losing a lot of blood. They put him on the gurney, and wrapped his arm up as they were preparing to leave. My grandmother was such an emotional wreck that she couldn't answer some of the questions. One of the guys asked me, "What's his date of birth, his name, age, and medical history?" while the other guys were keeping him stable in the ambulance. As he was done asking questions, they finally left. My mom then came to the house and asked my grandma, "What's going on?" She told my grandma that everything is going to be ok. Then my grandmother said to me, "Brandon, could you help me get dressed and find my important things?" Then she said, "Never mind, your mom is here. She can help me." While my mom was helping her find something to put on, she told her to call Don. She talked to Don and asked him to come to the hospital. My Aunt Juliette finally came and my mom said to her, "Juliette don't go in that bathroom, it's not a pretty sight." My aunt went near the bathroom and the tears began to flow. As I was getting my granddad's clothes to take to the hospital, my mom was in the den comforting my grandmother and aunt. So finally we got to the hospital and we sat in the emergency room for a very long time. My mom didn't go to work that day, but I still went to school because I needed to take a test in my Biology class. They took my granddad to ICU and he was there for a few days. The family was there until they got him stabilized. While I was at school, my mom and grandma went back home. My mom made sure that my grandma got some rest before we went back to the hospital. My mom cleaned up all the blood from the bathroom and the carpet. After I got home from school we went back to the hospital, and there we saw Mr. and Mrs. Rucker come through the door, and Mr. Rucker said to me, "How are you doing, Brandon? We are keeping your family in prayer." My Mom told them about what had happened. More church members had arrived, including Mrs. Rivers and Chaplain Jenkins, who was the Chaplain at the time. Then a few days later my mom told me that they were going to do surgery on his arm. The surgery was a success. They sent my granddad to different hospitals. First he was at Sentara Hospital, then the VA hospital, and then Mary Immaculate Hospital. Then he went back to the VA hospital. It was a very difficult and stressful time. I was a sophomore in high school around this time. Every day I would come home from school and my grandmother and I would go to the VA Hospital to spend a few hours with my granddad. While we were there, I would start some of my homework just to kill time and frequently go to the vending machine to buy some Cheetos and my favorite soda, Dr. Pepper. We would make sure he had dinner before we left to go home. Before we would leave, my grandmother would say a prayer. My granddad would look at me and say, "Brandon, make sure your grandma is okay." My granddad was in the hospital for about a month. He missed Thanksgiving that year, and it wasn't the same without him. It still isn't the same without him. He wasn't released until a few days after Thanksgiving. It was great seeing him back home. We went back to church and as soon as we entered the building, we received a standing ovation from the entire church. Mr. Jefferson gave my granddad a hug and said, "Welcome back, Pops." Mrs. Wilcox and others made their way over to greet us. When it came time to stand up and give a praise report, my granddad told the congregation what had happened. I could see a few church members crying while he was telling his story. He thanked everyone for their prayers, their cards, their visits, and their encouraging words. He said it made him feel good inside. He was very depressed during that time, but who can blame him. He'd been through hell and back. I miss him dearly.

There was another incident that occurred. This time it was with my grandmother. It all happened in 2008 on a Tuesday evening around 6:30 PM. I was cooking my granddad some fish and grits for dinner. He was watching *World News Tonight*, and I could hear my grandma saying, "I'm going to the store. I'll be right back." My grandfather replied, "Ok Julia, be careful." It was getting darker, and she hadn't come home yet. My granddad and I were getting worried. I was putting my shoes on and was getting ready to go see where she was. At this time I had my driving permit. I knew she was at Farm Fresh. While I was walking to my car, there was an Apple Red Impala right across the street, and then there was my grandma right behind it. I could hear the lady saying, "Mrs. West, is this your house?" and my grandma replied saying, "Yes, thank you so very much." My grandma forgot where she lived! She got out the car, and I brought in the two bags of groceries. My granddad was in tears saying, "Julia where have you been?" She replied, "I'm okay, Julius, I just went to the store." My mom came home not too long after this had happened. I told her that grandma got lost, and couldn't find her way back home. I told her that one of the neighbors had helped her get back home. My mom looked at me and said, "Brandon, the next time your grandma wants to go somewhere, you need to make sure you go with her, or run her errands for her." My grandmother is an independent woman who always did things on her own, but changes had to be made. That was the last time she ever got behind the wheel of a car. At that time my uncle Billy was running his cab business, and would frequently take my grandmother around as well as my mom to her appointments or any other place that she wanted to go. I would take her to places as well. My aunt Juliette would take her to get her nails done every Saturday or every other Saturday.

We later found out that my grandma was in the early stages of dementia. The doctor believed that when my grandmother suffered a concussion many years ago at NASA, it may have triggered her dementia years later. In the beginning, we all just thought it was old age. Elderly people have a tendency to forget things. People don't understand that dementia is a very horrible disease to have. You to have someone dress you, bathe you, change you, feed you, and so on. When a person is diagnosis with dementia, their sleeping patterns are off. They have a tendency to wander off and have no idea where they're at. You can't communicate with the person like you used to. It's like the person is a shell of their former self. As for my grandmother, we can still communicate with her. She isn't that bad off with the disease. She still takes medicine for her dementia.

On July 21, 2012, my grandma suffered a minor stroke on her left side. Her father, the late great Arthur C. Bryant, suffered a stroke many years ago on his left side as well. Strokes are very common on my grandmother's side of the family. It was early Saturday morning around 6:00 AM when DJ, my mom, and I took grandma to Sentara Hospital. There weren't that many people in the waiting room, so my grandma was quickly taken in the back to be evaluated by the doctors. Me and DJ sat in the waiting room watching the news about the incident that happened at the movie theatre. We then made our way to the cafeteria to get some breakfast. I sent texts to a few family members to let them know what happened. The family came to the hospital as they took grandma to her room. She was only in the hospital for a week before they transported her to Coliseum Park Nursing Home. While my grandma was at the Nursing Home, my cousins Juan, Spencer, and DJ stayed at the house. It was great having them all at the house at the same time. We went to go visit grandma before we went to Busch Gardens. Juan didn't go with us. He spent the day with Aunt Eleanor and Uncle Julius. We were at Busch Gardens all day long. We had a great time. We also went to the skating rink, and to the movies. Juan was with us this time. I wanted to take them to the Kings Dominion, but we didn't have enough time. Spencer had to go back to Charlotte, and Juan had to go back to Jacksonville. DJ was still here and my Uncle Jonathan came down to visit my grandma. As soon as he got to the house we went to see my grandma. We stayed there for a while, but had to leave because visiting hours were almost over. Jonathan, DJ, and I were driving around trying to find something to eat for dinner. Andrea's Pizza was closed so we couldn't get our steak and cheese subs. So we went to Chanello's pizza and got a jumbo-sized pizza. We went home and watched the Summer Olympics. We saw Gabby Douglas win a gold medal. I was very excited. On August 28, 2012, my grandma was finally released from the nursing home. That day was also her 57th wedding anniversary. When she got home I was excited to see her. Different nurses would come by the house to do different exercises with her so she could get the feeling back on her left side. It was very difficult to do because of her dementia, so was she was bedridden and still is. Her nurse, Shavanda, is always there with her from Monday through Thursday. Shavanda, has been her nurse for 3 years now. She has been a big help to my family.

In the summer of 2014 my grandma suffered a seizure for the very first time. It was around 7:00 AM in the morning. Juan and I were still sleeping. I usually got up around 7:30 AM or 8:00 AM. I heard a loud noise downstairs and my mom told me to call 911. The ambulance came and took her to Sentara Hospital. She stayed in the hospital for about 5 days. They gave her some medicine for seizures. My grandmother has had three seizures. The doctors would always up the dosage of her medicine to prevent it from happening again. As you can see, I've been through a lot in my life. In today's society there is absolutely no one in this world who can honestly say that they have no problems or worries in their life. Everyone has something to deal with and things to get over in their life. We all also have our own personal battles that no one knows about. As long as you are living and breathing on this earth, you will constantly have to fight battles and burdens in life. Some people are damaged by their hardships while others overcome them. Everyone knows that hardships are the most difficult things to deal with in life. Sometimes you may wonder, "How can a person physically, emotionally, and spiritually handle all of this? Where is God at in all of this?" I came to realize that he is *always* there. God was testing my patience and endurance, to see if I would give up or not. If I could get through this I could get through anything that life throws at me. Everything happens for a reason. You may not understand it, but sooner or later it will all make sense. You have to go through a lot of things to get God's blessings. God doesn't give the toughest battles to his strongest soldiers, but he takes the toughest soldiers through life's hardest battles. I always tell people, "If you can't be happy and joyful during the storms in life, then what makes you think you are going to be happy when you finally get out of it?" I truly believe that if anyone wants to hang onto life through the difficult times, you have to be strong and have a fighting spirit to not give up.

CHAPTER 5

FUTURE GOALS

It has been my desire in every part of my life to do different things, create my own path, and tread into unknown territory. I truly believe that if you plan on achieving success, setting goals is a very important thing. Having goals in life are not only giving you a clear perspective on things, but it helps you to organize your plans and allows you to give yourself boundaries. This is why I try to set goals for myself, whether it is just for today or for the rest of my life. A person needs to achieve goals in life before they can be called successful. I have many goals I would like to accomplish in my life. Some of these goals are personal while others are professional. I plan to move to Tampa, Florida, after I graduate from college in December 2015. While I'm in Florida I plan on finding a great job that makes me happy. I want stability in my job so I can raise my family without any financial issues. I'm not saying I need to make millions, but if God blesses me that way, I want enough so I can support my family. I cannot expect to have a family I can't afford. It's a beautiful thing to see your kids grow up before your eyes, and that is what I want in life. I will tell my kids that there is always going to be somebody out there who is prettier than you, more handsome, more successful, and so on. That doesn't mean you are *not* attractive or successful, only that some people are more blessed than you. All you need to do is be the best you can be. In life we're not all going to be winners. Sometimes you're going to lose, and when you lose, you'll be a better winner.

My kids will be raised with morals and values. I will teach my kids how to love themselves, and tell them to be whatever they want to be in life. I want them to make sure they keep God first in everything they do, and to not be afraid to talk to their parents about anything. Another goal of mine is to teach my kids to be grateful for what they have, and never compare their lives to anyone else's life. There is always somebody out there worse off than you. There is no need to envy or hate someone because they are blessed when in reality God has blessed you, and them as well. My kids will not walk out of my house looking like a mess. My kids will be well-kept! It's crazy seeing parents walk out of their house looking great, and their kids walking out of the house looking like trash.

I believe that you are successful in life if you have raised a family. I always tell people to establish yourself first before you start thinking about having kids or getting married. I've seen a lot of young people get married young, and then get divorced young because they thought they were ready. I'm not going to go that route. If I get married, it will be my first and *only* marriage. I want to get it right the first time! People want to rush into marriage, but haven't taken the time to mature properly. You might be saying to yourself, "Well, Brandon, my grandparents got married at a young age, and they are still together!" That may be true, but that generation was different back in those days. The men and women back in those days were a lot different from the men and women of this generation. Don't get me wrong; I have seen young couples in this generation last a long time, but just because it worked for them doesn't necessarily mean it will work for you. Sometimes I believe I was born in the wrong generation because I'm an old soul in a young body. My happiness in what I do in life is another a goal I have. There is no possible way that anyone can become successful if they are not happy with whatever passion or dream they have. If their passion is going to make them miserable, then they will never show 100% in their work. God has put a gift and talent in all of us. It's our job to find it and manifest into it. Your success is in your DNA. Nobody can make you see it. If you are reading this book, then I see a lot of potential in you. You need to stop having that negative mindset! Until you get over the hurt, pain, sorrow from broken marriages, horrible dating, baby daddy drama, baby mama drama, and personal issues in your life, then you can't receive the blessing and manifest into the destiny that God has for you. A lot of people are bitter because they can't figure out what God has put inside of them. If you don't know what God has put inside of you, then you need to pray, and ask God to show you who you are to yourself. If your gift is to be in the fashion business then do it. If your gift is fitness, music, singing, dancing, whatever, then do it.

My goal in life is to simply be happy and content with life. I believe that should be everyone's goal in life. A lot of people feel that they are lost in this world. They work extremely hard, breaking their backs every single day, and it seems like they don't get anywhere. The real reason why people have this problem is because they really didn't spend enough time thinking about what they really want out of life. After all, would you go on a journey without much thought into what you really want out of life? I believe the answer is no. Setting goals in life is a great way for thinking about your future, and to encourage yourself to turn your dreams and goals into reality.

My other goal is to stay active in the gym, and staying healthy. I love going to the gym. The gym is my second home where I can clear my mind and thoughts. Health problems run rampant in my family. Some of these health problems are diabetes, heart problems, strokes, colon cancer, stomach cancer, prostate cancer, kidney failure, high blood pressure, high cholesterol, and more. These are the reasons why I try to stay healthy. Seeing my grandparents have different bags of medicine that they needed to take was kind of depressing. My granddad would always tell me, "Brandon, take care of your health. If I knew I would have all of these health problems I would've changed some of things in my diet." I have other goals that I want to keep accomplish, but you will just have to wait and see about those.

CHAPTER 6

MY THOUGHTS ON SOCIETY

We live in a society where it seems like everyone is self-absorbed. No one is being generous, and no one desires to give back. People want to be in the limelight, and don't seem to care how they get there or who they step on in the process. Be careful how you treat others on your way to the top, because you never know who you are going to meet again on your way back down! You may need their help.

There is constant pressure on women to be overly sexual. There is no more respect for the modest woman. In order for a woman to be noticed, the clothes she wears have to be tight and short, not to mention that her shape has to be just right or she really won't get any man's attention. Ladies, I want to tell you that you don't need to be half naked in order for a REAL MAN to notice you. Believe it or not, a lot of men want their women to respect themselves. I remember my Grandmother used to always say, "Leave it to a Man's imagination of what you have." Men often admire and appreciate a woman who knows how to carry herself with confidence. Women who dress half-naked are women I can't take seriously. There are ways of looking nice without showing everything. It seems like some women don't wear bras, slips, or even panty-hose anymore. There is no reason for you to have your breasts hanging all out, and wearing a dress way up your butt-crack. Have you ever seen a woman at a funeral or at church wearing a dress that is so short that every time she stands up she is always pulling her dress down? It's like the material of that dress can't get any lower. You already have a big butt anyway. Even if you don't have a big butt, it still looks trashy. If you dress like a hoe, you are going to get treated like a hoe. You dress like a lady, you are going to get treated like a lady. It's just that simple. So ladies, your appearance and how you dress speak volumes. I always say what you put out there is what you get. Wear something appropriate that fits your body the right way next time.

Another issue that goes on in society is seeing guys walking around sagging their pants. It looks stupid, to be honest with you. I've even seen old men walking around sagging their pants trying to look young again. I believe some guys do it because they want to give off that tough-guy vibe, or they are desperately trying to fit in. Either buy pants that fit you, or buy a nice black leather belt. If you can spend $200 on a new pair of Air Jordans, then I know you can easily go to Walmart and purchase a nice black belt. It's very unprofessional to walk around with your pants to the ground. Nobody wants to see what color underwear you have on. Some guys don't even know where sagging of the pants originated. It originated in the prisons. It was a way of telling the other inmates that you were available for sex! That's what sagging your pants really means. Maybe that will be a wake-up call for a lot of guys to pull their pants up.

I also want to talk about how we as black people don't support each other. The reality is that some blacks seem to generally hate each other, and it's a shame. It's not so much about black people hating each other, it's just that some hate themselves, so they go around hating other people, and it rubs off on others. You have that black woman whose man cheats on her, and she tells her friends, "Girl, black men ain't nothing. All they do is lie and cheat." The same thing goes for some guys saying, "All women do is whine and complain all the time." We are the only race that continuously and repeatedly bash our own people. We don't know what it is to be united. First of all, love yourself and then love your brothers and sisters. Some blacks don't know how to do that. Instead, some of them are always trying to bring someone down. It's like feeding off of negativity, feeding off letting others down. You don't want to see somebody move up the ladder to be successful and positive. You want to see what the media portrays us to be.

Always hating somebody is another issue with black people. Some blacks thrive on hating, and spreading rumors about others. It's ridiculous. Instead of you helping each other to achieve greatness, to achieve success, some blacks don't try to help at all. Some of them want to destroy each other. Automatically doubting that people are going anywhere in life. Always talking about what people can't do. This is the reason why we are not going anywhere as a culture of people. We are our own worst enemy. I want to see more empowerment rather than competition in the black community. This issue has nothing to do with white people. This has been an issue within the black community for a very long time. Also, black people need to understand that just because things don't go our way doesn't necessarily mean that it's racism.

Ladies, I have another issue with you. Stop calling yourselves "bad b-----s." Any woman on this planet who believes that calling yourself a bad b---- is a badge of honor has some serious emotional issues. Then you want to get mad when a man calls you one. Personally, I find calling anyone a bad b----, a sexy b---, or whatever is degrading, regardless of whether or not it is said in a joking way. It's very depressing that using it has become so casual and accepted. That just goes to show you how disrespectful this society has become. How can you demand respect from others if you are degrading yourself? It's very illogical, to be honest with you. You teach people how to treat you. If I said it once, I'll say it again. RESPECT YOURSELF. Being known as a successful and respectable woman is a lot better then referring to yourself as a bad b----.

Colorism is another issue I have with society. Colorism is more common with black women. Too many blacks are brainwashed to think that you have to be light skinned to be considered beautiful, which makes other women more insecure about themselves. Dark skinned women are just as beautiful as light skinned women. There is no law that says dark skin is ugly. The media just doesn't want to show beautiful dark skinned women. Instead, they want to show the blue-eyed, blonde-haired, light skinned women, making the majority of women believe that is the standard example of beauty, which we all know is false. Colorism has poisoned the black community to the point where we are being racist and discriminatory within our own race! That's what hurts the most. Some men are disowning darker women, and some women are disowning darker men. Believe it or not, there are some parents out there hoping and praying their child doesn't come out looking dark. You have black women, and sometimes even black men, bleaching their skin to look more attractive to society. They are literally poisoning their own bodies because of the slave mentality that has been put inside black people for so many years, and as well as the media showing black people that being light skin makes you superior.

Now don't get me wrong, light skinned women have a hard time as well. They may not have it as bad as dark skinned women, but they have problems as well. I know a few light skinned women that told me they were bullied as kids because the other girls thought they were trying to be better than everyone else. Some of them were bullied because others thought that they were stuck up. This light skinned girl that used to ride my bus back in high school was saying that people assumed she was mixed race just because she was light skinned. She said they told her that she had a white person's lips. Since when does having certain facial features determine what race you belong to? I just don't get it. All I have to say is black women are beautiful. It really doesn't matter if you are light skinned, dark skinned, or even brown skinned. Black is beautiful, period.

A few years back I came to realize that black people are not the only ones who deal with colorism. This Asian guy at the gym told me they regard lighter Asians differently than darker Asians. It's also the same for Hispanics, and even Irish people. I just think that Colorism is plain ignorant, and it needs to stop.

Another issue I would like to discuss is this: Why do people have a problem with interracial dating? It doesn't make sense to me. Everything is about race. Can't it just be called dating? You are responsible for your own actions and happiness. Do what's best for you. We can't control the behavior or actions of other people, and unfortunately there will always be someone who is going to not only disagree, but be vocal about interracial dating. I hear some of these negative reactions coming from several black women. I hear some black women say, "He can't handle a strong black woman. He had to go get a white woman to walk all over." That has to be the dumbest thing I ever heard in my life. Again, black women don't seem to mind if they see other black women dating outside the race. It is up to you both to just focus on each other and your relationship. Ignorance can't be avoided, but it can be ignored. Why does skin color even matter anyway? If a white man is with a black woman, and a black man is with a white woman, then who cares. There are more problems in this world to worry about than to care about two people in a relationship with each other that are simply different because of their skin color. Love is love. If you found True Love with someone who is loyal, faithful, and puts up with you, then why does the fact that their skin is different change anything? Just leave people alone, and let them do their own thing. Interracial dating is not just black and white, because you have Hispanic/Black, Asian/Black, White/Hispanic, White/Asian, and so on. We have to learn how to move forward! We can't blame this generation for what happened 400 years ago. I love interracial relationships. I see more and more each and every day.

In the words of Brandon West: Live, love, forgive, and be happy knowing you can overcome anything if you put your mind to it and put God first.

ABOUT THE AUTHOR

Brandon L. West is a twenty-five-year-old native of Hampton, Virginia. He graduated from Kecoughtan High School in 2008 with Honors. He will graduate from college in December of 2015 with a degree in Information Systems Technology. Brandon possesses wisdom beyond his years. He loves to encourage others to follow their dreams and be successful in life. Brandon is a very understanding person, and is easy to talk to. His expertise is in helping others overcome adversity. Whether you encounter his message through his books or speaking events, your life will undoubtedly be enhanced.

To learn more about Brandon L. West, please visit
www.brandonlwest.com.

www.ingramcontent.com/pod-product-compliance
Lightning Source LLC
Chambersburg PA
CBHW071112090426
42737CB00013B/2574